STATE PROFILES

IDAHO

BY BETSY RATHBURN

BELLWETHER MEDIA • MINNEAPOLIS, MN

Blastoff! Discovery launches a new mission: reading to learn. Filled with facts and features, each book offers you an exciting new world to explore!

BLASTOFF! UNIVERSE

BLASTOFF! Beginners
GRADE K

BLASTOFF! READERS
GRADES 1-3

BLASTOFF! DISCOVERY
GRADE 4

This edition first published in 2022 by Bellwether Media, Inc.

No part of this publication may be reproduced in whole or in part without written permission of the publisher.
For information regarding permission, write to Bellwether Media, Inc.,
Attention: Permissions Department,
6012 Blue Circle Drive, Minnetonka, MN 55343.

Library of Congress Cataloging-in-Publication Data

Names: Rathburn, Betsy, author.
Title: Idaho / by Betsy Rathburn.
Description: Minneapolis, MN : Bellwether Media, Inc., [2022] |
   Series: Blastoff! Discovery: State profiles | Includes bibliographical
   references and index. | Audience: Ages 7-13 | Audience: Grades 4-6 |
   Summary: "Engaging images accompany information about Idaho.
   The combination of high-interest subject matter and narrative text is
   intended for students in grades 3 through 8"– Provided by publisher.
Identifiers: LCCN 2021019641 (print) | LCCN 2021019642 (ebook) |
   ISBN 9781644873830 (library binding) | ISBN 9781648341601 (ebook)
Subjects: LCSH: Idaho–Juvenile literature.
Classification: LCC F746.3 .R27 2022 (print) | LCC F746.3 (ebook) |
   DDC 979.6–dc23
LC record available at https://lccn.loc.gov/2021019641
LC ebook record available at https://lccn.loc.gov/2021019642

Text copyright © 2022 by Bellwether Media, Inc. BLASTOFF! DISCOVERY
and associated logos are trademarks and/or registered trademarks of
Bellwether Media, Inc.

Editor: Kate Moening   Designer: Jeffrey Kollock

Printed in the United States of America, North Mankato, MN.

TABLE OF CONTENTS

SHOSHONE FALLS

SHOSHONE FALLS
TWIN FALLS

A family pauses on their hike along the Snake River **Canyon**. Before them, the Snake River cuts through tall stands of dark rock, disappearing into the distance. After taking in the view, they continue on. The sound of rushing water grows louder as they approach the top of the canyon wall.

BRUNEAU SAND DUNES STATE PARK

CITY OF ROCKS NATIONAL RESERVE

CRATERS OF THE MOON NATIONAL MONUMENT AND PRESERVE

IDAHO BOTANICAL GARDEN

Finally, the family takes the last step. They are atop a tall cliff covered in green shrubs. Over a steep drop, Shoshone Falls rages. At 212 feet (64.6 meters) tall, it is one of the highest waterfalls in the United States. This is beautiful Idaho!

WHERE IS IDAHO?

Idaho is in the **Pacific Northwest**. At 83,569 square miles (216,443 square kilometers), it is the 14th biggest state. Boise, the capital, is in southwestern Idaho. It is the most populous city in the state.

Six states and one Canadian **province** form Idaho's borders. Washington and Oregon are to the west. Idaho shares its southern border with Nevada and Utah. To the east is Wyoming, and Montana is to the northeast. In the north, Idaho borders a 45-mile (72-kilometer) stretch of British Columbia, Canada.

WASHINGTON

OREGON

NEVADA

IDAHO PANHANDLE

One special part of Idaho is the Idaho Panhandle. This long, narrow part of northern Idaho looks like the handle of a frying pan!

BRITISH COLUMBIA, CANADA
COEUR D'ALENE
MONTANA
SNAKE RIVER
N
W
E
S
BOISE
IDAHO
IDAHO FALLS
WYOMING
TWIN FALLS
UTAH

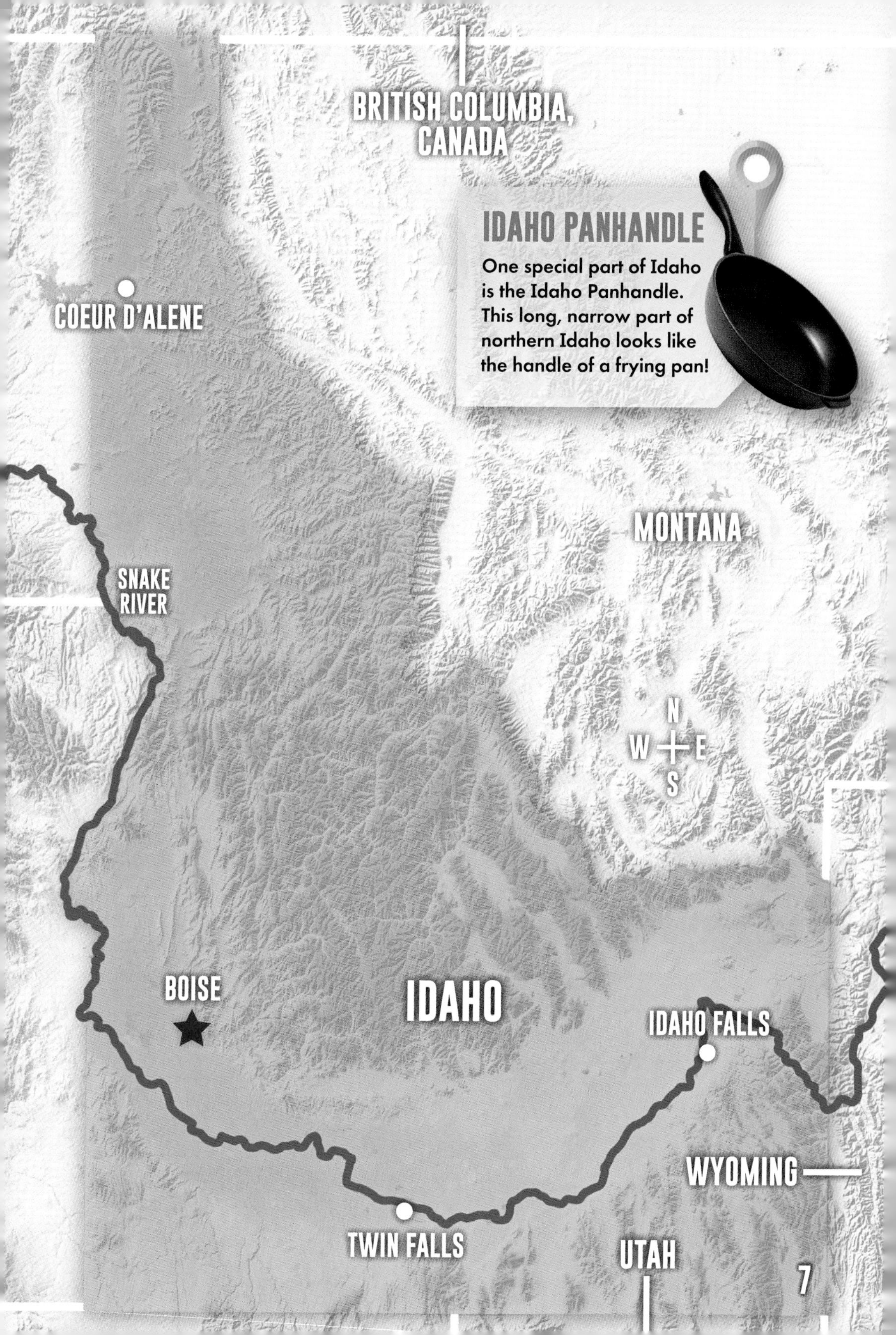

COEUR D'ALENE
DANCERS

People have lived in Idaho for at least 10,000 years.
Among the earliest groups were the Clovis, Folsom, and Plano
cultures. By the 1800s, the Coeur d'Alene, Nez Percè, Paiute,
and Shoshone people lived in the area. In 1803, President
Thomas Jefferson ordered explorers to head west. Meriwether
Lewis and William Clark arrived in Idaho two years later.
They were the first Americans to visit.

Idaho became part of the Oregon **Territory** in 1848. Many people passed through the area. In 1863, the Idaho Territory was established. Idaho became the 43rd state almost 30 years later, in 1890!

NATIVE PEOPLES OF IDAHO

COEUR D'ALENE

- Original lands in Idaho's northern panhandle
- More than 2,190 enrolled in the Coeur d'Alene Reservation
- Also called Schitsu'umsh

SHOSHONE-BANNOCK

- Original lands in southern Idaho
- About 5,850 enrolled in the Fort Hall Reservation
- Also called Newe (Shoshone) and Northern Paiute (Bannock)

KOOTENAI

- Original lands in northeastern Idaho
- 165 enrolled
- Also called Ktunaxa

NEZ PERCÈ

- Original lands in Idaho's central panhandle
- More than 3,500 enrolled in the Nez Percè Reservation
- Also called Nimiipuu

WESTERN SHOSHONE AND NORTHERN PAIUTE

- Original lands in southwestern Idaho
- Over 2,000 enrolled in the Duck Valley Reservation
- Also called Newe (Shoshone)

Idaho is part of the Columbia River **Basin**. Forests blanket much of the state. Mountain water drains into the state's many rivers, including the Snake River. They flow toward the Pacific Ocean. The towering peaks of the Rocky Mountains cover northeastern Idaho. The tallest mountains rise more than 12,000 feet (3,658 meters) high!

SNAKE RIVER

ROCKY MOUNTAINS
COLUMBIA PLATEAU
YELLOWSTONE NATIONAL PARK

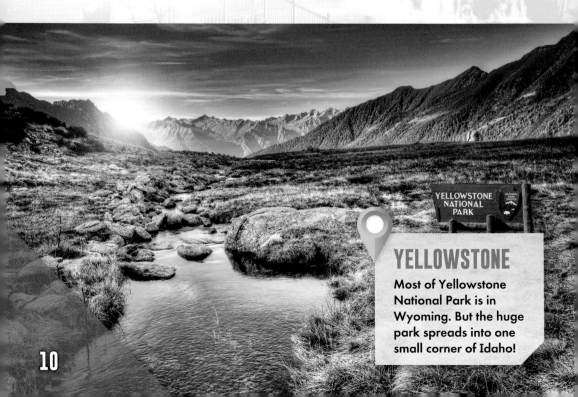

YELLOWSTONE NATIONAL PARK

YELLOWSTONE

Most of Yellowstone National Park is in Wyoming. But the huge park spreads into one small corner of Idaho!

SAWTOOTH MOUNTAINS
ROCKY MOUNTAINS

SPRING
HIGH: 61°F (16°C)
LOW: 38°F (3°C)

SUMMER
HIGH: 85°F (29°C)
LOW: 55°F (13°C)

FALL
HIGH: 62°F (17°C)
LOW: 39°F (4°C)

WINTER
HIGH: 39°F (4°C)
LOW: 24°F (-4°C)

°F = degrees Fahrenheit
°C = degrees Celsius

IDAHO'S FUTURE: DISAPPEARING SNOW MELT

Idaho temperatures are warming due to climate change. This means mountain snow often melts in early spring instead of summer. Less water then drains into Idaho's streams. This will lead to more droughts and wildfires in the coming years.

Idaho's mountains have cool summers and snowy winters. People must watch out for blizzards and avalanches. Southern Idaho sees heavy winter snows and dry summers. Forest fires are common in dry weather. In western Idaho, the flat Columbia Plateau usually has mild weather.

11

Animals walk, fly, and swim across Idaho! Bighorn sheep roam the eastern highlands looking for tasty grass. Mountain lions often trail behind them, hoping to catch their next meal. Mountain bluebirds sing from the trees. Grizzly bears and gray wolves also prowl Idaho's mountains and forests.

Peregrine falcons are Idaho's state **raptor**. These fierce birds look out for gophers, chipmunks, and other food. Many fish swim in Idaho's rivers and lakes. Steelhead trout return from the ocean to lay eggs in Idaho's rivers each year!

PEREGRINE FALCON

MOUNTAIN LION

GRIZZLY BEAR

STEELHEAD TROUT

BIGHORN SHEEP

12

MOUNTAIN BLUEBIRD

Life Span: up to 10 years
Status: least concern

mountain bluebird range =

LEAST CONCERN	NEAR THREATENED	VULNERABLE	ENDANGERED	CRITICALLY ENDANGERED	EXTINCT IN THE WILD	EXTINCT

With around 1.8 million residents, Idaho is one of the least populated states for its size. About 7 out of 10 Idahoans live in cities. Most have **ancestors** from Europe. People with Hispanic backgrounds make up the next-largest **ethnic** group, followed by Native Americans. Many Native Americans live on **reservations**, though others live in Idaho's towns and cities. A small number of Asian Americans and Black or African Americans also live in Idaho.

BASQUE BACKGROUND

Many people with a Basque background live in Idaho. Their ancestors are from a small region of Spain and France along the Bay of Biscay.

LAKE COEUR D'ALENE

FAMOUS IDAHOAN

Name: Picabo Street
Born: April 3, 1971
Hometown: Triumph, Idaho
Famous For: Alpine ski racer and Olympic gold medalist who competed in the 1994, 1998, and 2002 Olympic Games

Around 100,000 Idahoans were born outside of the United States. Many recent immigrants moved to Idaho from Mexico, Canada, the Philippines, China, and Kuwait.

Boise is in southwestern Idaho along the Boise River. French fur traders arrived in the area in the early 1800s, seeking shelter from the hot, dry **plains**. Later, a **gold rush** led to a population boom. **Fort** Boise was built to support the many miners. In 1864, Boise became Idaho's capital.

FORT BOISE, 1849

BOISE GREENBELT

CITY OF TREES

Long ago, few trees were found in the land around Boise. But many trees have been planted in the city. They have been brought from all over the world. Today, Boise is known as the City of Trees!

Today, more than 200,000 people live in Boise! The city is home to government buildings, large businesses, and many neighborhoods. People enjoy biking through parks along the Boise Greenbelt. The Boise Art Museum attracts visitors with its paintings and sculptures. There is plenty to see and do in Boise!

INDUSTRY

LOGGING

In the 1800s, fur trading made up most of Idaho's economy. Many early traders came from the Hawaiian Islands. In the 1860s, a gold rush created a mining boom. Most early miners came from China. Miners needed a lot of wood to make equipment. This led to growth in logging.

IDAHO'S FUTURE: TECHNOLOGY BOOM OR BUST

Idaho is home to many technology companies. Some worry these companies will leave as they grow. There are not enough people in Idaho to work for them. If the companies leave, other Idaho businesses may struggle.

Today, only a few gold mining companies remain in Idaho. But logging continues in Idaho's forests. Farming is important, too. Idaho farms grow potatoes, barley, and many other crops. Many Idaho companies process food and **manufacture** parts for computers and medical devices. People in **service jobs** work at Idaho's many restaurants, hotels, and ski resorts.

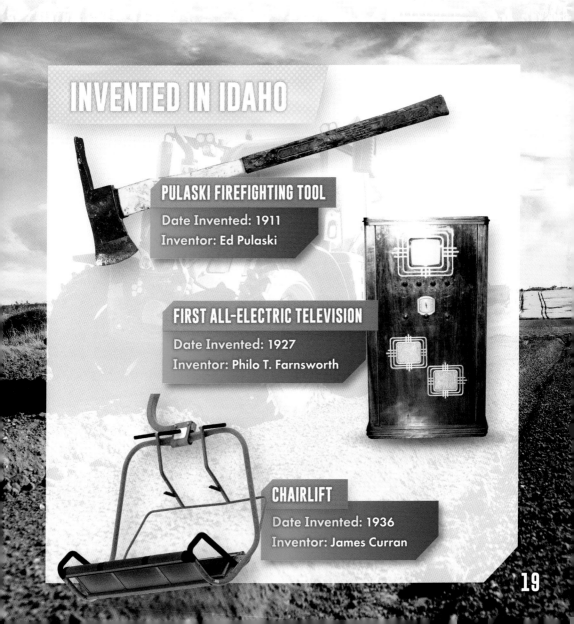

INVENTED IN IDAHO

PULASKI FIREFIGHTING TOOL
Date Invented: 1911
Inventor: Ed Pulaski

FIRST ALL-ELECTRIC TELEVISION
Date Invented: 1927
Inventor: Philo T. Farnsworth

CHAIRLIFT
Date Invented: 1936
Inventor: James Curran

PAELLA

Idaho's food is shaped by its people! A large Basque population means that hearty stews are popular. *Paella*, a rice and fish dish, is also common. This meal is served from a large dish at the center of the table. Everyone takes their share!

Idahoans enjoy many special local sweets. In summer months, people eat huckleberries right off the bush. This state fruit also sweetens pies and ice cream. An Idaho ice cream potato is vanilla ice cream shaped like a baked potato. The outside is dusted in cocoa powder, and it is topped with whipped cream!

HUCKLEBERRY PIE

IDAHO ICE CREAM POTATO

FRENCH FRIES

ABOUT **32** FRIES

Have an adult help you with this Idaho classic!

INGREDIENTS

4 large potatoes, scrubbed and peeled

olive oil or cooking oil

salt

DIRECTIONS

1. Preheat the oven to 350 degrees Fahrenheit (177 degrees Celsius).

2. Cut each potato lengthwise into long strips.

3. Put the fries in a mixing bowl and toss with oil.

4. Place the fries in an ungreased baking pan.

5. Bake for 20 minutes. Remove the fries from the oven and turn. Return to the oven and bake for another 10 minutes, or until golden.

6. Sprinkle with salt and serve hot.

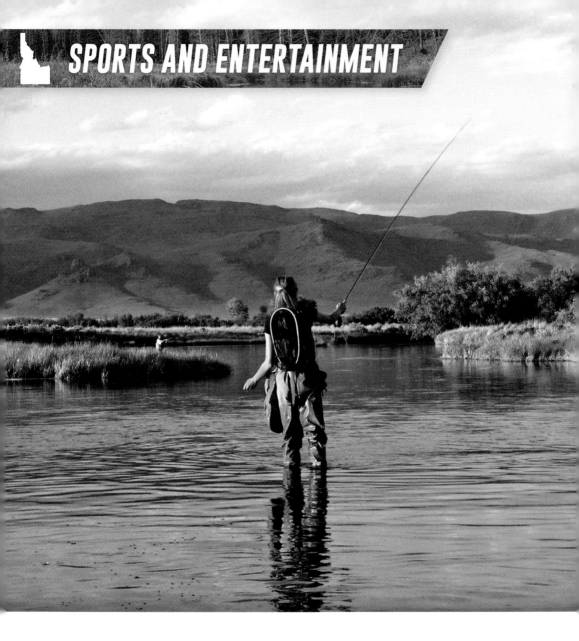

Idaho is full of activity! Many local museums show off Idaho art and history. In Boise, people look for outdoor paintings and sculptures across the city. People come to Idaho Falls to watch concerts on the Snake River. Fishing, camping, and hiking are popular throughout the state. Many people soak in Idaho's **hot springs** when the weather is cool!

Idahoans also love local sports. People cheer on the Idaho Steelheads hockey team and the Idaho Vandals college football team. Many people also play baseball and soccer. Skiers and snowboarders can be found on snowy mountains. Idaho is full of fun things to do!

SKI TIME

Idaho has 18 ski resorts. The highest, on Bald Mountain, rises more than 9,000 feet (2,743 meters).

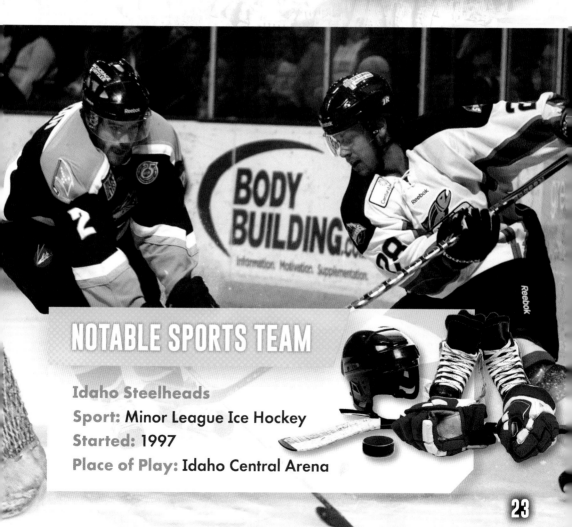

NOTABLE SPORTS TEAM

Idaho Steelheads
Sport: Minor League Ice Hockey
Started: 1997
Place of Play: Idaho Central Arena

Many fun events fill Idaho's calendar. Every five years, the Jaialdi festival celebrates Idaho's Basque people. **Traditional** food, music, and dancing draw thousands of visitors. Each August, people enjoy music, dancing, and rodeos at the Shoshone-Bannock Indian Festival.

Other festivals celebrate Idaho's food. In Idaho Falls, Idaho Spud Day shows appreciation for the Idaho potato. The festival is held every September. People play tug-of-war, watch parades, and compete in potato baking contests! The Donnelly Huckleberry Festival celebrates Idahoans' favorite fruit. Visitors listen to music, eat, and browse crafts. Idaho's festivals celebrate all that makes the Gem State great!

JAIALDI FESTIVAL

IDAHO SPUD DAY

IDAHO TIMELINE

1860

Gold found in Idaho leads to the Idaho Gold Rush

1805

Explorers Lewis and Clark enter Idaho

1848

The Oregon Territory, which includes Idaho, is established as part of the United States

1864

Idaho Territory's capital is moved to Boise

1834

Fort Boise is built

1868

Shoshone and Bannock people are moved to the Fort Hall Indian Reservation

26

1936

The Shoshone-Bannock people establish their constitution

1890

Idaho becomes the 43rd state

1976

The Teton Dam collapse leads to widespread flooding

2014

Eighth & Main, Idaho's tallest building, is finished

1924

Craters of the Moon National Monument and Preserve is established

Nickname: The Gem State

Motto: *Esto perpetua*, Latin for "Let it be perpetual"

Date of Statehood: July 3, 1890 (the 43rd state)

Capital City: Boise ★

Other Major Cities: Coeur d'Alene, Idaho Falls, Twin Falls

Area: 83,569 square miles (216,443 square kilometers); Idaho is the 14th largest state.

Population

1,839,106 (2020)

STATE FLAG

Idaho's flag is bright blue. In its center is a yellow circle, called the Great Seal of the State of Idaho. The center of the circle holds two people. One is a miner, representing the state's important mining history. The other is a woman who represents equality and justice. Between them is a shield that shows Idaho's mountains and trees. An elk head rises above the shield, showing Idaho's wildlife. On the ground are two groups of fruits and vegetables. These show the importance of farming in Idaho.

INDUSTRY

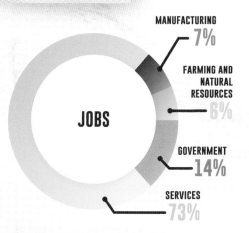

JOBS

- MANUFACTURING **7%**
- FARMING AND NATURAL RESOURCES **6%**
- GOVERNMENT **14%**
- SERVICES **73%**

Main Exports

computer parts

paper products

aircraft parts

cheese

cattle

potatoes

Natural Resources

timber, silver, lead, phosphate

GOVERNMENT

Federal Government

2 REPRESENTATIVES | **2** SENATORS

ID

USA

4 ELECTORAL VOTES

State Government

70 REPRESENTATIVES | **35** SENATORS

STATE SYMBOLS

STATE BIRD
MOUNTAIN BLUEBIRD

STATE TREE
WESTERN WHITE PINE

STATE FLOWER
SYRINGA

STATE HORSE
APPALOOSA

ancestors—relatives who lived long ago

avalanches—events in which a large mass of snow, ice, rock, or dirt falls down a mountainside

basin—the area drained by a river

canyon—a deep and narrow valley that has steep sides

cultures—societies that hold the same beliefs, arts, and ways of life

ethnic—related to a group of people who share customs and an identity

fort—a strong building where soldiers live

gold rush—the rapid movement of Americans to the western part of the country after gold was discovered in the mid-1800s

hot springs—places where hot water flows out of the ground

immigrants—people who move to a new country

manufacture—to make products, often with machines

Pacific Northwest—an area of the United States that includes Washington, Oregon, and Idaho

plains—large areas of flat land

plateau—an area of flat, raised land

province—an area within a country; provinces follow all the laws of the country and make some of their own laws.

raptor—a large bird with a hooked beak and sharp claws that eats only meat

reservations—areas of land that are controlled by Native American people

service jobs—jobs that perform tasks for people or businesses

territory—an area of land under the control of a government; territories in the United States are considered part of the country but do not have power in the government.

traditional—related to customs, ideas, or beliefs handed down from one generation to the next

AT THE LIBRARY

Hyde, Natalie. *Rocky Mountains Research Journal.* New York, N.Y.: Crabtree Publishing Company, 2018.

McDaniel, Melissa. *Idaho.* New York, N.Y.: Children's Press, 2019.

Wilson, Wayne L. *The Shoshone.* Kennett Square, Pa.: Purple Toad Publishing, 2020.

ON THE WEB

FACTSURFER

Factsurfer.com gives you a safe, fun way to find more information.

1. Go to www.factsurfer.com.

2. Enter "Idaho" into the search box and click 🔍.

3. Select your book cover to see a list of related content.